My "P's & Q's" (poems and quotes): Volume 2

Darvin Kerby

BookLeaf
Publishing

India | USA | UK

*To that invisible friend who I never see but I know
is always there. Distance matters not for it only
takes a solitary thought and you are there.*

Preface

Simple words are the stepping stones of our conversations and communications. They build a girded and solid foundation of friendship.

Acknowledgment

Humble thanks to a grand Creator that bestows particular abilities to each one of us and to find that ability and use it.

Alibi is why a man didn't do something. Motive
is why a man did something.

******

Each erroneous act we commit cripples the
sovereignty of our conscience.

******

Each moment granted to us is genuinely precious
So, may our dance with time be sincerely
gracious.

******

It's a glowing mirage
Like misty applause
Or a ghostly corsage
A subtle camouflage
Vaporizing massage
A reality's sabotage
Delusional barrage
Or the hazy collage
I see this entourage
Many things because
It's a glowing mirage

******

Now when they lay me down to sleep
My soul is the Lord's to take and keep
There will be nothing much left to leave
Maybe memories for those who grieve
Or possessions of some value or worth
Trinkets gathered during life on earth
Maybe a name carried through the age
Something for others to peer and gauge
But it matters not to those who've left
Those are things for the sad and bereft
When a dying man draws his last breath
And he looks across the way at death
And his time remaining will be no more
As he's taken through eternity's door
He surrenders all he owns and owes
He cannot keep what he knew or knows
And all he ever was or would have been
Whether sweet or bitter it all must end

******

Loneliness can be the coffin you exist in or it can
be the resurrection of a new start.

******

We may shed silvery tears to achieve golden
dreams. But those silvery tears will be the
glorious luster of the glittering gold. While pearls
of joy and rubies of gladness are the resplendent
brilliance and iridescent glow of those golden
dreams.

******

Indecision leads to inability.

******

It's like a moonlight sonata
Knowing you and I oughta
Be swaying to them beams
Watchin the silvery gleams
Dancin in a midnight glow
Footsteps be droppin slow
Like a ballerina's pirouette
Waltzin a late night minuet
Lightning does its showing
Our feet in rhythm flowing
While the thunder applauds
A mesmerizing monologue
An ensemble of pearly light
Splashin in the starry night
Splatters of tiny dewdrops
Greeting dawn on rooftops
Kissing nighttime goodbye
The morning sun rises high
Fleeting shadows run away
Making room for a new day
Sleep sound my dear friend
Until we meet to do it again
Sun-kissed, moon-caressed
Will always remain the best

******

There are three mugs sitting on the shelf
One filled with the thought of days gone by
Precious memories of invaluable wealth
Recollection of things money can't buy
One of prismatic glittering tears wept
Those liquid prayers only God can hear
These silent cries in the heart are kept
Listening to what isn't said is most dear
One filled with hopes of a tomorrow bright
A future filled with expectations is power
Grants today a radiant promising twilight
Fading, blending into a dawn's new hour
So whatever your mugs on a shelf are
May your vessels be full and overflowing
Whether a flask, decanter, cup or a jar
Keeping these embers of emotion aglowing

******

It's easy to forget a man exists
To place no value upon his life
It insults a soul to be dismissed
Remove hope with tongued knife
To be forgotten is a punishment
It's a picture taken with no image
Dark shadows of abandonment
To be emptied by forced primage
Unnecessary burdens of silence
Echoing through an empty heart
Unseen scars made by voidance
The arrows sink like poison darts
When another's reality is ignored
The price is great and costs dear
Loneliness a man cannot afford
To exist and presently disappear
A man's journey is truly his own
His path should be well-adorned
Not a sparse landscape of stone
Sticks, weeds, thistle and thorns
There are no tariffs on kindness
No fees imposed for friendship
That always helps to remind us
The walk of life is wonderful trip

******

Will you stand beside my grave and weep
Or will you simply gloss over my absence
Will missing me touch your heart deep
Or will you be wrapped in blanketed pretense
Will you wonder of me with heavy reflection
Or just muse over with nonchalant indifference
Will memories bring any personal connection
Or will they contribute to a trifling insignificance
Will you feel hollow emptiness or loneliness
Or will my death bring you a sweet release
Will reminiscing bring you some happiness
Or now you can rest in a repose of peace
Will there be any sacredness in your tears
Or will silence be your redeeming stance
Will echoed words be music in your ears
Or is my passing away just a minor
circumstance
When this storm comes without a warning
for certainly every man's days are numbered
May there be more happiness than mourning
And smiles of many happy things wondered

******

Two Morrow

Today we stand between what was and what is to be
Each moment we are in contrast to twain
possibilities
Energetic vibrations of a balance of time and eternity
Between canvases of living our lives and
immortality
We're a Creator's masterpiece yet a work in progress
We have our failures but still can achieve success
We're purposely designed to make rational choices
Rhetoric or noise can't confuse us but the voices
We can err to fault with remorse or accept lessons
We can be stoic or have essence of our expressions
We can be both avid dreamer and a steady
performer
We can be an arch revolutionary or active reformer
But whether yesterday or long into a distant future
We longingly gaze in two-morrow's grand picture

******

Within each facet of time, we weave a thread of
eternity. The fabric of eternity covers the past,
present, and future. Everything that has happened in
the past, each thing that occurs in the present, and
anything that will take place in the future are sewn
together with the threads of eternal tapestry.

******

Seeking or searching for something is only as valuable and viable as the motive which drives it. This reveals the true intent and personal desire of the seeker.

******

Loneliness is not presided over by any season
Grief is not a practitioner of the passing times
Sorrow comes to teach us all by persuasive reason
Misery and melancholy come in maddened
rhymes
Feeling of deep distress caused by feeling lost
Misfortune suffered becomes a heavy taskmaster
Heartfelt anguish storms like a tempest-tossed
Causing rainfalls of a hopeless and emotional
disaster

******

Would you hold me and never let me go
These are the things a heart needs to know
Will you dance with me in the evening light
These are the things a heart must have right
Would you kiss me with the kisses so sweet
These are the things a heart needs to beat
Would you carry my worries like your own
These are the things a heart must be shown
Would you love me to the ends of all time
These are the things a heart needs to rhyme
Just seeing your smiling face as we meet
This is what my heart needs to be complete

******

Between the Rock and that hard place
Needing mercy and praying for grace
Appealing to God and pleading a case
Fear stands tall with a shadowy trace
Worries rise at an incredible pace
Causing a lost heart to rapidly race
But God's eternal love we can embrace
And every difficulty the Lord does erase
When we in the Spirit behold His face

******

In the deepest recesses of the heart is where a soul
makes its most earnest pleas.

******

Tomorrow's history is today's mystery.

******

Goodbye is the clasp that seals that priceless
necklace of remembrance around your neck.
Laden with those pearls of memories and
recollections.

******

Is it really a talent that I possess
Or do I just have curious passion
Is it something that others I bless
Or what I do is just selfish fashion
Can I caress ears with expression
Or is it just a pursuing fascination
Can others see muted suggestion
Or is it all merely my imagination
Is my written words soft and deft
Or are they just a clanging noise
Do they lift hope and spirits aloft
Or are words just my employees
None can be artist without a gift
A gift is not unless it's been given
Something setting a mind adrift
Writing, a tale lent from heaven

******

It is the one that never leaves
That almost just about sneeze
When someone's face crinkles
Ready with tissue for sprinkles
Then there's a hearty bless you
When you are totally through
A sneezer holds against a hope
Having a languid-lipped grope
Will this be the big pika achoo
Will there be only one or two
Could it be that achoo bacca
Like a cry of a newborn alpaca
Stander-by waits with patience
With ge sund heit dissertation
You can feel it and they see it
Begs for the sneeze not to quit
And audience gasps collective
From a sneezer's odd perspective
Will there be a uniform cheer
When achoo falls on their ear
Or will a creased face statement
Turn into a huge disappointment
As an almost just about sneeze
Becomes one that never leaves

******

My heart grows silent
From weariness within
Withdrew and reticent
What comes has been
Like the passing storm
When the rain ceases
A rainbow's lovely form
Clouds scattered pieces
How the mind traverses
Across galaxies in thought
An imagination rehearses
And loneliness is life's lot
What's the measurement
Of all depth, width, height
Of a heart's contentment
With a rareness of delight
But I find total happiness
And deep perfect solitude
Oh complete peacefulness
In humble prayer renewed

******

An ingénue with twain entities
Poetess of captured dual soul
Filled with life and possibilities
Visions set to reach lofty goal
She is the epitome of fire and ice
Personification of all passions
Embodiment of desire or vice
Proper with naughty fashions
She can be a vocal resonance
Or yet deep and secret silence
Symbol of pertinent relevance
Or of defiance and of violence
Dyad spirits diverging into one
Traveling a road less traversed
Traits from the moon and sun
Living a life full and well-versed
She's the essence and element
She's the question-and-answer
She is effect and development
She's the song and the dancer
She is a pioneer and innovator
But yet she's settled and strong
She's entertainer and liberator
She's pause of an angelic song
She can be her own best friend
Or can change into her own foe
So what a stranger does intend
Be of honor or you'll be of woe

******

Four hundred and forty-four
Could one ask for any more
It removes doubts and fears
It pays tribute to your tears
It's an assurance of direction
Reaffirms guided protection
It encourages perseverance
Through each circumstance
With focus and determination
With a measure of dedication
It aids with current approach
And helps avoid reproach
It maintains positive planning
To bring clear understanding
A sign of love and wholeness
Turning emptiness to fullness
It's not just numeric sequence
It comes to pledge allegiance

******

I may never find a cure for a rare disease
Nor I may never walk the regions of space
But I can hear the music playing in the trees
As I watch branches dance certain with grace
I may never sail upon the seven blue seas
Nor I may never fly across the universe
But I see the beauty spread across the galaxy
Each star knows its part and well-rehearsed
I may never understand the concepts of science
Nor I may never find any fame or fortune
But I've discovered solitude within silence
And I have lived a life to its fullest portion
I may have never found upon this old earth
What others seek so desperately to find
But I've found something beyond any worth
Eternal life with life's worries left behind

******

I'm swimming in a river of debt
A wide and engulfing tributary
Assured promise to not forget
For an account extraordinary
For it's not money that's owed
It is an obligation of gratitude
For all that has been bestowed
Pledge of honor daily renewed
Privileged covenant to uphold
Debt is relinquishing poverty
It can be prison to those souls
Any repayment is not robbery
Thanks, a fire from fresh coals
Truth is, a sun never proclaims
To an earth below what's given
The bounty of its golden flame
It's a life giving gift from heaven
Nor is the moon above envious
Of the lights of a twinkling star
But each other grants obvious
Compliments on how each are
Interest paid on an appreciation
For acts of kindness and favor
Compensate on grand occasions
With a valiant robust endeavor
One can only attempt to repay
The kind and benevolent deeds
Any person can receive in a day
And filling someone else's needs

Earnest and sincere recompense
Not by paying back but forward
And to do so sparing no expense
Charity puts men's steps in order

******

In the beauty of the sunrise the dappled palette of colors are cast upon the canvas of sky. Waiting for the artist to complete the masterpiece of the day. That golden pearly glow of the first rays of sunlight cast across the darkened horizon. The blazing yellow fingers of the sunbeams wrap themselves around the protruding edifices that stand tall from the shadows. The morning dawns with awe-inspiring sensations of glowing lights and colors. Morning has come!

******

May your skin be so thin that others can see the
holy candle of the Lord shining within.
May your skin be so thick nothing cannot dim the
wick of the burning heart set in the candlestick.

******

Compassion is amplified exponentially if we find
a common connection with the person needing
help. It moves us from just doing something for
someone to standing in their shoes and
understanding their plight.

******

Being on purpose is no accident.

******

When the rainbow meets the hurricane.
It is a sunny day before a stormy rain
This is when sweet joy meets sorrow.
It is peace today needed for tomorrow
It is solid ground on which we stand
When things feel like shifting sand
God's eternal promise and pledge
An assurance when on life's edge
Wrapped in our Comforter's arms
Before the ringing of danger's alarms

******

If the moon was a heart
Its light bathes every part
Every virtue soaked in love
From that silvery river above
Each beam would be a beat
Each ray echoing so sweet
No desire or passion hidden
Secrets of dark is forbidden
And as the moon does glow
Its love the world shall know
For when it shines this way
It is bright enough to be day

******

Whoa is me

Whoa is a small command given to slow down
It is the shepherd's cry to the sheep of his flock
It's a cry to simply stop and take a look around
It is God's voice for us to ask, seek, and knock
It is a cry from heaven to grab your attention
A call from God's Holy Spirit for us to be still
To grant to you from all troubles a redemption
True peace and contentment won't happen until
We stop and let go of all our haste and hurry
When we cease and refrain we will find rest
When we bring an end all our cares and worry
Then the stillness and quiet you'll be blessed

******

God does not have a heart that is wild and free
But He has an eternal love for all of humanity
God is not reckless abandonment
you see
But a perfected order in measured degree
God told man not to eat from that certain tree
But man that violated that granted liberty
From dawn of time God gave free agency
But men caught by Satan's luring captivity
In turn God provided the miraculous
crucial key
God sent His son born in humble nativity
Greeted by a resounding angelic symphony
Christ becomes a door for men and eternity

******

The hidden recesses of life takes notion
Behind every wrinkle are hidden emotion
Each line tells the stories of toil or peace
Memoirs etched deeply and never cease
Within every crinkle is a smile and laughter
Where hopes and dreams do long after
In those fading depths of sheerest joy
It's love's disport that does happily employ
A bright twinkle sparkling in your eye
Like stardust gleaming in a night sky
Someone wished upon a shining star
From depths of a heart there you are

******

Faith changes feelings. Faith changes fear. Faith changes fallacy. Faith changes falsehood. Faith changes fable. When all these factors fall before faith then we can follow the Faithful One with familiarity of trust and firmness of conviction.

******

In moments of deep despair
When things are up in the air
You will find those who care
The friend who is really rare
Will be the one who is there

******

The last beat of His heavy-ladened heart echoed across the universe.
The last sigh of His sacred breath rang through the galaxies. The last hallowed words He uttered reverberated through the heavens.
The last drop of His holy blood that hit the earth resonated through the constellations. Death was the final door He had to cross as a man but He became that door that opened up heaven to mankind.

******

You cannot see the sadness of sin until you
discover the goodness of God.

******

A heart's tic tac toe
With the Xs and Os
All lined up in a row
No one really knows
If they are for show
For kisses to bestow
And hugs we do owe
Grace and virtue flow
To hearts we pray go
Reward of Xs and Os

******

It's not my fault you say
But I see it another way
You chose to walk away
That horrid frightful day
I couldn't make you stay
And thinking back today
What else could we say
It was just a price to pay
Emotion had gone astray
Feelings were on display
Parts we both had to play
Our passion in mortal clay
Decision makes one sway
But now bright as a sunray
Our memories are in decay
A heart at your foot will lay
In the end, all left is to pray

******

The vast majority of successes in life are achieved
through a simple want to. Because I want to then
I am able to. The vast majority of failures in life
are achieved through a simple I don't want to.
Because I don't want then I am not able to.

******